Comedy Scripts

The Two Ronnies

Ronnie Barker
adapted by Bill Ridgway

Macmillan Education

This text is simplified and adapted from the original scripts by Ronnie Barker first published in book form by Hodder and Stoughton Ltd as *It's Goodnight From Him*

Original text © Ronnie Barker 1976
This adaptation © Bill Ridgway 1986

All rights reserved. No reproduction, copy or transmission of this publication may be made without written permission.

No paragraph of this publication may be reproduced, copied or transmitted save with written permission or in accordance with the provisions of the Copyright Act 1956 (as amended).

Any person who does any unauthorised act in relation to this publication may be liable to criminal prosecution and civil claims for damages.

First published 1986

Published by
MACMILLAN EDUCATION LTD
Houndmills, Basingstoke, Hampshire RG21 2XS
and London
Companies and representatives
throughout the world

Designed by Milford Hurley

Typeset by Vine & Gorfin Ltd, Exmouth, Devon
Printed in Hong Kong

British Library Cataloguing in Publication Data
Barker, Ronnie
The Two Ronnies.—(Comedy scripts)
1. Readers—1950-
I. Title II. Ridgway, Bill III. Series
428.6'2   PE1126.D4
ISBN 0-333-40390-8

Acknowledgement
The author and publishers wish to thank the BBC for giving permission to use the photographs included in this book

Contents

Hear Hear	RC RB	1
A Greengrocer's Shop	RC RB	4
The Wedding	Vicar Man Girl	8
Gentleman Caller	Householder Intruder Young Man (1 line)	12
The Case of Mrs Mace	RC RB	16
Reaching Agreement	RC RB Jones	19

Hear Hear

(*RB sits at desk. There is a large sign on the wall – 'HEARING-AID CENTRE'. Enter RC. He approaches the desk.*)

RC: Is this the hearing-aid centre?

RB: Pardon?

RC: Is this the hearing-aid centre?

RB: Yes, that's right, yes.

RC: I've come to be fitted for a hearing-aid.

RB: Pardon?

RC: I said I've come for a hearing-aid.

RB: Oh, yes. Do sit down. I'll just take a few notes. Name?

RC: Pardon?

RB: Name?

RC: Crampton.

RB: Pardon?

RC: Crampton.

RB: Oh, Crampton.

RC: Pardon?

RB: I said Crampton.

RC: Crampton, yes.

RB: Right, Mr Crampton. Now, I take it you are hard of hearing.

RC: Pardon?

RB: I said, I take it you're hard of hearing.

RC: That's right.

RB: Which ear?

RC: Pardon?

RB: Which ear?

RC: The right.

RB: Pardon?

RC: The right ear.

RB: Ah. Could you cover it up with your hand please? (*He does so.*): Now, can you hear me?

RC: Pardon?

RB: Can you hear what I'm saying?

RC: It's very faint.

RB: Pardon?

RC: It's very faint.

RB: I can't hear you.

RC: Pardon?

RB: Try the other ear. (*RC covers it.*) Now what's that like?

RC: I still can't hear you.

RB: Can you hear me?

RC: Pardon?

RB: Yes. You really do need a hearing-aid.

RC: I thought so.

RB: Pardon?

RC: You can't hear *me*, either, can you?

RB: Pardon?

RC: Why don't *you* wear one?

RB: You're still very faint.

RC: A HEARING-AID! Why don't *you* wear one?

RB: I *am* wearing one.

RC: Pardon?

RB: Pardon?

RC: I said, 'Pardon?'

RB: No, I said, 'Pardon!'

RC: Oh, never mind – I'll get some new teeth. (*He goes out.*)

A Greengrocer's Shop

(RB is just finishing serving a woman, tipping brussels sprouts into her shopping basket. RC enters, and approaches RB.)

RC: Two pounds of potatoes, please.

RB: Right, guv. *(He weighs them out.)* Lovely, these are.

RC: Yes, they look good. Could I have them in a bag, please?

RB: What?

RC: They're a present for someone.

RB: Oh. Er...

RC: You know – a bit of coloured paper, a nice box, something like that. Makes all the difference, doesn't it?

RB: Oh, it does, guv, yeah. I don't know what I've got...

RC: Well, leave it for a bit, there are some more things I want. Have you got anything for an old aunt?

RB: Well...

RC: She sits on her own a lot and doesn't do much.

RB: How about some prunes?

RC: No. I don't think so. It's not the sort of thing you give as a present, is it? No – I know. A cabbage. That's right. A nice big cabbage.

RB: Right – how's that one? *(Shows him a cabbage.)*

RC: Fine, she'll like that. Now then, what about Mum?

RB: Mum? Your mum?

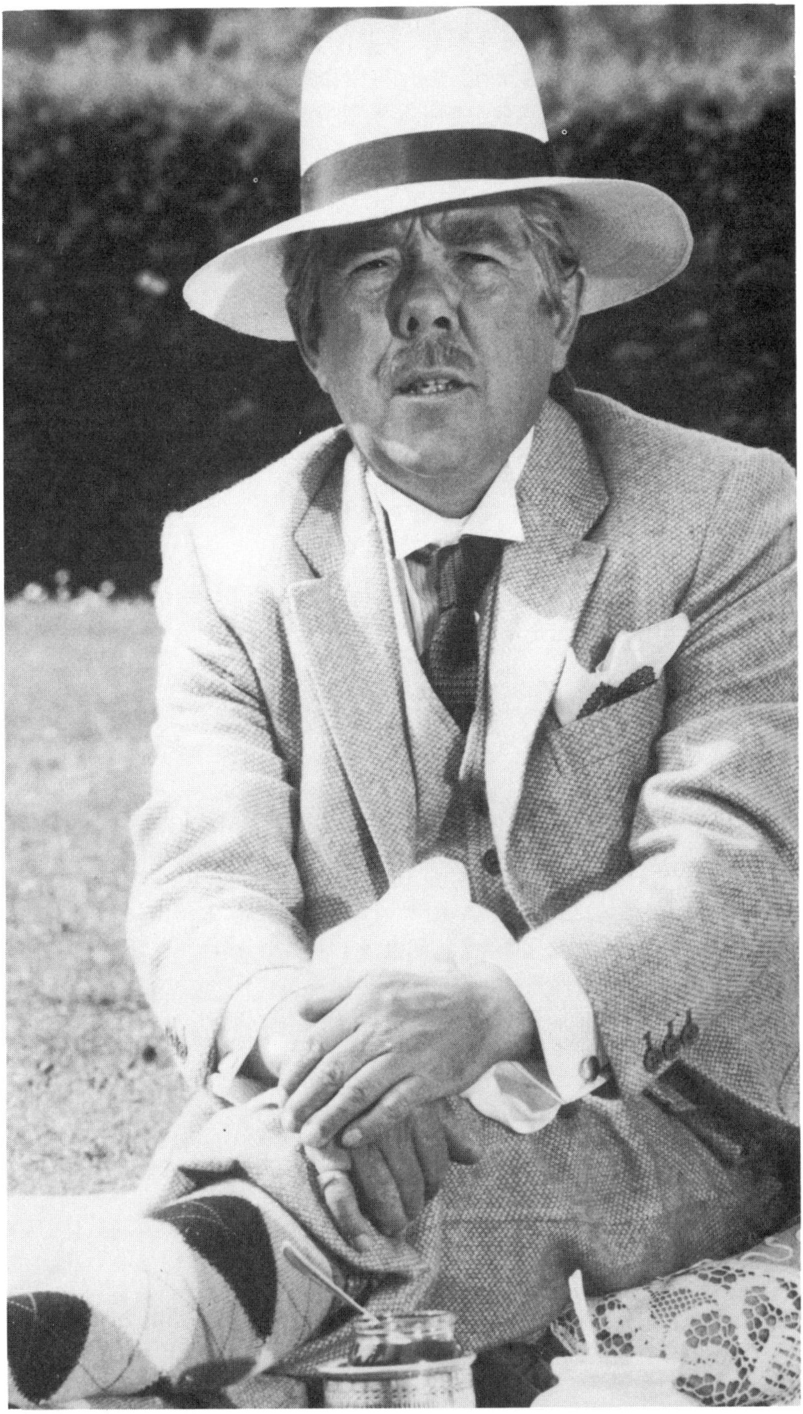

RC: Yes. She's hard to choose for. She's got everything.

RB: (*Thinks for a second then –*) I bet she hasn't got any chestnuts.

RC: Yes, she has. Plenty.

RB: Tomatoes?

RC: No, I gave her those last year.

RB: Oh.

RC: She's still got some left.

RB: I've got it. What about two pears, set in straw, side by side. A sort of gift box?

RC: It's not a bad idea.

RB: (*Showing him*) Look at those. They'd be a real treat for anybody's mum.

RC: Now, then. What about Uncle Willy?

RB: What's he like?

RC: Well, he's a very heavy smoker.

RB: What about a few artichokes. That would be a laugh.

RC: (*Laughing*): Yes, it would. That's great. (*RB starts to put some into a bag.*) Just a minute, what's funny about an artichoke?

RB: Hearty Choke. Heavy smoker. You see? Arti-choke! (*He coughs and splutters.*) Choke! Hearty ... how about a marrow?

RC: Yes, all right. Now, do you send vegetables by telephone?

RB: No.

RC: You see, I've got these relatives in Australia, and they miss their spring greens at Christmas.

RB: Don't they get spring greens in Australia?

RC: Only in summer, you see. That's the way it works out. Well, never mind. Have all these things sent round to this address, would you? (*Gives him a card*.) Nice to get my Christmas shopping done all in one go, isn't it?

RB: Yes, isn't it?

(*RC goes, then comes back.*)

RC: I am silly. I bought all those things, and I haven't got myself anything for lunch today. How much are the flowers?

The Wedding

(*The bridgroom waits. The 'Wedding March' is played as the Bride comes in on the arm of her father, followed by little girl bridesmaids. The Vicar faces them. The bride arrives and the music stops.*)

Vicar: We are here to join together this man and woman...

Man: Excuse me.

Vicar: (*Whispering*) What's the matter?

Man: This isn't the one.

Vicar: Which one?

Man: This isn't the one I'm marrying.

Vicar: Not the one you're marrying?

Man: No. (*To girl*) Are you? I've never seen her before. Have I?

Girl: (*Shaking her head*) No.

Vicar: Are you sure?

Man: Of course I'm sure.

Girl: Everyone's looking at us.

Vicar: Well – what's gone wrong?

Girl: Could you get on with the wedding? Everyone's listening.

Vicar: Well, I can hardly...

Man: Yes, carry on for a minute while we have a think.

Vicar: Oh, all right... (*Vicar carries on while man and girl talk.*)

Girl: What are we going to do?

Man: Well, we've got to stop it, haven't we? I mean . . .

Girl: I can't, I can't. I've waited months for this moment. I've been looking forward to it.

Man: Well, so have I. I mean – well, we both have, but we've been looking forward to it with different people, haven't we?

Girl: But my mum will go mad if it all falls through. She's got all the sandwiches and sausage-rolls ready.

Man: But getting married isn't just about sausage-rolls, is it?

Girl: She sat up all night in a chair so she wouldn't spoil her new hair-do. Anyway, I don't know what you're really like, do I?

Man: Well, I'm just like anybody else, aren't I?

Girl: You're very little.

Man: I'm not little. It's you that's big.

Vicar: (*He's come to the end of his words.*) Have you thought about anything yet? I've come to the part where there's no going back.

Girl: It's just that we don't know if we're right for each other. It's a question of size.

Vicar: Size should have nothing to do with it.

Man: You'll have to give us another minute.

Vicar: I'll tell you what – I'll give them a hymn to be going on with. (*Speaks aloud.*) We will now sing hymn number 798, 'A Stranger is with us, shall we let him in.'

(*The people start to sing.*)

Girl: I don't really mind short men.

Man: As a matter of fact, I love tall girls.

Girl: I'm not all that tall, you know.

Man: You are to me.

Girl: What do you think then? Shall we make a go of it?

Man: Where would we live?

Girl: Oh, my dad's bought me a new house.

Man: Well that's all right then. OK Vicar, you can carry on.

Vicar: We'll just wait until the hymn finishes.

Man: All right, then. (*Looks at girl.*) We *have* met before, you know. At school.

Girl: Were *you* at the same school?

Man: We were in the same class.

Vicar: Do you, er . . .

Man: Robin Clifford.

Vicar: Do you, Robin Clifford . . .

Girl: Robin Bates!

Vicar: Do you, Robin Bates . . .

Man: Robin Clifford.

Vicar: Robin Clifford, take . . .

Girl: Old Mother Thompson's!

Vicar: Take Old Mother Thompson . . .

Girl: Mavis Jean.

Vicar: Take Mavis Jean, for your wedded wife, to have and to hold . . .

(*Vicar carries on.*)

Man: I always said I'd marry you – ever since I was nine. I never thought it would be like this. (*In answer to the Vicar*) I do.

Vicar: And do you, Mavis Jean, take Robin Clifford...

Man: Here – what about the man you were going to marry?

Girl: I never liked him much. Anyway he was only marrying me because he felt sorry for me. (*To Vicar*) I do.

Man: What do you mean, he felt sorry for you?

Girl: Well, he had his own way with me.

Man: Well, that can't be helped. It doesn't mean to say you've got to marry him, does it?

Girl: Well, I thought it was only right. I mean...

Vicar: I now pronounce you man and wife.

Girl: (*Showing him the six bridesmaids*) I've got to give this lot a father, haven't I?

(*Man faints.*)

11

Gentleman Caller

(*An intruder stands there; a little man, with a big bag and a guilty face.*)

Householder: (*Seeing intruder*) Good God!

Intruder: Ah! You're in. Good.

Householder: So are you, it seems. What are you doing in my dining room?

Intruder: Er – I'm – I'm just . . . Higgins. I'm just Higgins. Justin Higgins. I'm a solicitor.

Householder: You're not a solicitor.

Intruder: I'm not a good solicitor, no. To be honest – I'm fairly rotten, as a solicitor. My partner deals with most of the work. I'm more the tree-cutting side of the firm.

Householder: You're the what?

Intruder: I cut down trees. Got any trees you want cutting? Any work in the garden?

Householder: What?

Intruder: Well, let's put it this way – how are you off for compost? Got plenty, have you?

Householder: I haven't got any.

Intruder: Right. I'll put you down for a sack. Now what about seeds? Plants for the garden?

Householder: Now just a minute! This is a flat. And it's nine floors up.

Intruder: Well, have you thought of sunflowers? They're nice and tall. You could get the people downstairs to water them.

Householder: You know nothing at all about gardening.

Intruder: Oh, don't I?

Householder: Well, do you?

13

Intruder: I don't; no. But my brother's great. He's got green fingers.

Householder: Oh, he's the gardener.

Intruder: No, he works in a stamp factory. But to be honest I really came to see you because of this pain in my back.

Householder: You're talking a lot of rubbish.

Intruder: The pain in my back and the pain in my head.

Householder: You're a crook.

Intruder: A crook?

Householder: What have you got in that bag?

Intruder: Sandwiches. Just sandwiches for my lunch. One beef, two cheese and tomato.

Householder: In a bag that size?

Intruder: And a gallon of beer.

Householder: You're lying.

Intruder: Yes, I am.

Householder: You admit it?

Intruder: Yes, I do.

Householder: I thought as much.

Intruder: It's two beef and one cheese and tomato.

Householder: (*Grabbing bag*) Come on, let's have a look.

Intruder: How dare you! Leave the bag alone! Those are my sandwiches.

Householder: (*Looking into bag*): What's this? Books? Have you been stealing books from the bookshops?

Intruder: Certainly not. I've just been to the library.

Householder: These are brand new!

Intruder: Yes. They're from the brand new library in Station Road.

Householder: (*Reading*) The Home Encyclopedia. Eight books in a set. I could do with these.

Intruder: Well, you're not having them. I took a lot of trouble pinch... getting those. They're very difficult to get. They're £15 a set in the shops.

Householder: Now look. Here's £10. Now either you take the money and clear off, or I shall pick up the 'phone and get the police. And that would drop you right in it. Wouldn't it?

Intruder: That reminds me – do you want that bag of compost or not?

Householder: Come on, out! (*He pushes him toward the door.*)

Intruder: You haven't heard the last of this! I'll get my brother on to you. (*He is pushed out of the door but pokes his head round again.*) Not the one with green fingers, the one who's a solicitor!

Householder: Out! (*Moving slowly away.*) Or I'll 'phone the police.

Intruder: All right – I'm going.

(*The door is slammed in his face. Outside the door a younger man is leaning against the wall.*)

Young Man: How did you get on, Jack?

Intruder: All right, Harry. Sold another set.

The Case of Mrs Mace

(A Police Station – a room or office within the Station itself. RB as plain-clothes detective sits at a desk. RC enters.)

RC: Good day, Inspector Jay.

RB: Morning, Dorning. Any news of the Girder murder?

RC: Yes sir. He's been shot at Oxshott. Bagshot got him with a sling full of buckshot.

RB: He's a good shot, Bagshot. Well, you must be pleased that it's all over.

RC: The relief is beyond belief, chief. Now my mind is a blank. And I've only got you to thank.

RB: All right. Now it's still morning, Dorning, and I'm glad to hear your head's clear: it means there's more space for the Mrs Mace case to take its place.

RC: The Grace Mace case? Have they traced the face? *(Points to Photofit picture on wall.)*

RB: No – and the nightdress is still missing.

RC: Is she sure it was the right nightdress? She's not mistaken about what was taken?

RB: How come, little chum?

RC: Well, to the beautiful Mrs Mace, all her nightdresses are made for love and lovingly made. Whatever she wore, she'd still be a bonny, beautiful nightie-full.

RB: Yes, she's a grand lady to have as a landlady.

RC: What a laugh to be asked to inspect her, inspector. Any suspects to inspect?

RB: Yes – two. Two of them are actors who live with Grace – at her place in the Chase. One is Len Mighty, known for his charmers, farmers and men in pyjamas. and the other is Roger Mainger, who once played a stranger in a film with Stewart Grainger called *Deadly Danger*.

RC: May I add another to your list?

RB: Who?

RC: Sergeant Bodger!

RB: What? That constable from Dunstable? You must be crazy.

RC: It's just a theory, dearie. May I sit down?

RB: Please – make yourself comfy, Humphrey.

(*RC sits.*)

RC: It's just that Bodger has got a face like a fit: which fits the face on the Photofit in the first place, and he's often to be found at her place in the Chase, filling his face with fish.

RB: Fish?

RC: Fried by Grace – Mrs Mace. Mostly plaice.

RB: But what about Len Mighty? He's there nightly – isn't it more likely? She looks very flighty in her nightie – he's the sort of toff that might try to pull it off.

RC: But there's something you don't know.

RB: I don't?

RC: No. I've spoken with Roger.

RB: Roger?

RC: The lodger.

RB: Oh – Roger Mainger, who played the stranger with Grainger.

17

RC: He says he saw Len take the nightie. He was looking through the keyhole in Mrs Mace's bedroom door.

RB: He dared to stare through there? Would he swear he saw Len Mighty take the nightie?

RC: He'll do plenty of swearing. No wonder he was staring – it was the one she was wearing!

RB: What? Surely not!

RC: He pulled it over her head. She went red, and he fled. He locked himself in the shed, and wished he were dead. She was going to phone her cousin Ted, but felt dizzy in the head, so she lay on the bed and went red.

RB: So you said. Roger is a liar!

RC: Have you any proof?

RB: I've seen where Mrs Mace sleeps. It's an attic! So the story about pulling the nightie over her head is false. He would have to pull the nightgown down! There's no headroom in her bedroom!

RC: So Roger's lying! Then he must be the one! So ends the disgraceful Grace Mace case.

RB: (*Picks up the phone*) I'll just tell the Chief Constable – Hello, sir – we've solved the Mace case. I'm happy to tell you that Len is innocent, and so is Sergeant Bodger. Yes, sir. In other words – it was not Len Mighty who lifted the nightie, but Roger the Lodger, the soft-footed dodger, and not Sergeant Bodger, thank God!

Reaching Agreement

(*Four old men at a board meeting. They all look alike. One – Mr Green – is asleep.*)

RB: Now gentlemen, we have called this meeting because we are worried that the company is not doing all it can to keep the firm ahead. Southern Safety Pins Ltd. is well-known, and sales are steady. But we can do better and we have to think of ways of making more money – not to put too fine a point on it.

RC: But surely, Hopkins, if we don't put too fine a point on it, the safety pin won't do up. And that's your trade up the spout. That would mean the end of the firm.

Jones: How about making the spout more round? I'm sure that by and large, people prefer a round spout.

RB: Well, large people would, certainly. I should have thought it was a question of taste.

RC: I disagree. It doesn't matter what things taste like, as long as it says 'Tasty and fresh' on the packet. Mark my words.

Jones: That's not a bad idea. Mark the words in red on every tin. They'll sell like hot cakes.

RC: Perhaps we could put ovens in the supermarkets to keep the cakes hot. That would put us streets ahead of the other firms.

RB: Well, I suppose street-trading is something we could think about. Although the council would probably put the tin hat on that.

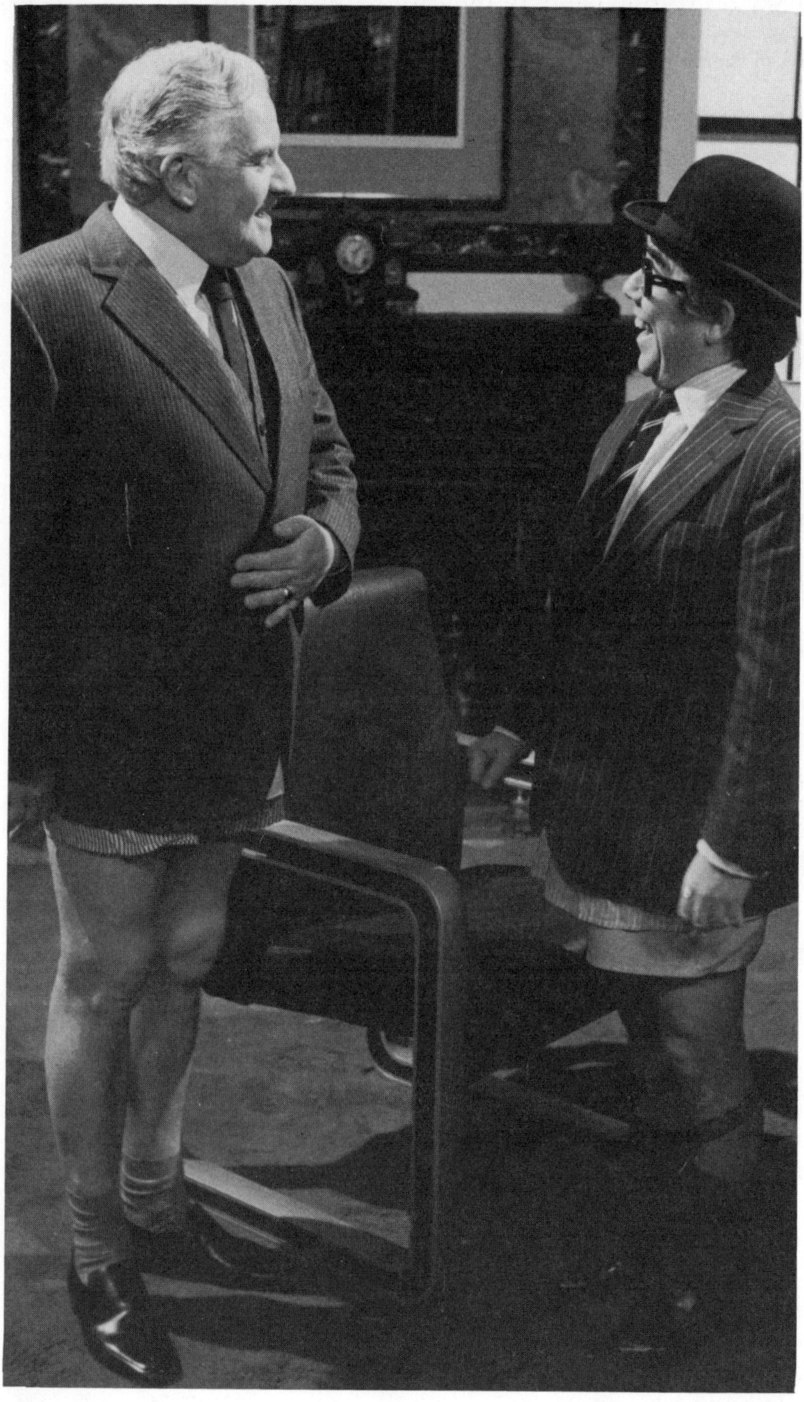

RC: Hardly likely to help trade, I think. I mean, if I saw a man standing by an oven in the street with a tin hat on, I'd think it was a little odd.

RB: Well, they could wear signs saying 'I am not a little odd'. And they could push things through letter boxes, for the housewife.

RC: Yes, letter boxes are worth looking into. Perhaps we could try it out in some key places.

Jones: Well, the best key place I know is under the mat, by the back door.

RB: True. You know, these keys could open up all sorts of things with houseowners.

RC: And if we get the owners to open up their houses, people could come in for a small charge. We'd beat other firms on their own ground.

RB: I think it will work – and not only on our own ground, but when we are playing away as well. Of course, we need someone to really get the team fit. The question is who's best?

RC: He used to be a famous footballer. Georgie Best.

RB: Then he's the man we want! Make him the boss, and get people to open their houses.

RC: Do you think we can do this? Get the public's houses open?

RB: What's the time?

RC: Ten to twelve.

RB: Is it? Oh yes, they must be open by now. Come on, I'll buy you one.

(*They all get up and wake up Mr Green.*)

RB: Come on Green, the pubs are open.

RC: We're going to vote for Georgie Best.

(*Mr Green gets up.*)

Jones: Well, that's that then.

RC: Yes – nice to feel you've got something done, isn't it?

RB: Quite. All you have to do is get round a table and talk about it.

(*They go out to the pub.*)